THE MEANINGS OF MODERN ART

by JOHN RUSSELL

Art Critic, *The New York Times*

VOLUME 3

HISTORY AS NIGHTMARE

THE MUSEUM OF MODERN ART, NEW YORK

I. Gustave Moreau
Salome Dancing before Herod (detail), 1876
Musée Gustave Moreau, Paris

It was at the Paris Salon of 1876 that Moreau had the greatest public success of his career, with a version of *Salome Dancing before Herod*. He had been obsessed with Salome: not merely with Salome dancing, but with Salome taking her ease, Salome planning her crime, Salome gloating over the head of St. John the Baptist, and Salome terrified by the ghost of that same head as it floats in the air before her. *Salome Dancing before Herod* inspired a famous passage in the novel *A Rebours* by J. K. Huysmans. Moreau's Salome was the personification, as Huysmans saw it, of "the monstrous, indifferent, irresponsible, impervious beast who, like the Helen of Antiquity, poisoned all who approached her, all who saw her, all who touched her."

2

One of the key remarks of this century occurs in a very long novel which was begun in 1914 by an Irish writer who had yet to make a name. James Joyce was the writer, the novel was *Ulysses,* and the remark was all of 11 words long. "History," said Joyce's Stephen Dedalus, "is a nightmare from which I am trying to awake."

I take "history" to mean, here, a sense of the past as something that determines the present to an intolerable degree. To be born in a certain place, at a certain time, and of a particular parentage, can be a disadvantage from which it is impossible to recover completely. I take "nightmare" to mean, here, the state of mind defined in 1931 by Ernest Jones, the eminent psychoanalyst and biographer of Sigmund Freud. Jones described the classic symptoms of nightmare as "agonizing dread, a sense of oppression or weight at the chest which alarmingly interferes with respiration, and a conviction of hopeless paralysis." A sense of history as nightmare, thus interpreted, is as severe an affliction as can be wished upon us.

Yet we can all think of times at which that sense was mandatory among intelligent and sensitive people. The calendar of the recent past is full of such times, and very often they are linked to particular places: Prague in 1968, Dallas in 1963, Budapest in 1956, Hiroshima in 1945, Leningrad during the siege of 1941–43, Pearl Harbor in 1941, Paris in 1940, Berlin in 1933. To be aware of what was going on in those places at those moments was to experience in our waking life the terrors attributed in 1834 by a Scottish savant, Dr. Robert Macnish, to the nightmare state: "The whole mind is wrought up to a pitch of unutterable despair; a spell is laid upon the faculties which freezes them into inaction; the wretched victim feels as if pent alive in his coffin, or overpowered by resistless and unmitigable pressures."

At such times, and in the face of such thoughts, we realize how high van Gogh was aiming when he said that he wanted his paintings "to retain their calm even in the midst of catastrophe." Art and literature are there at such times to steady us: to remind us that night thoughts, even when warranted, are not the whole of life. But art and literature are also there to remind us of aspects of existence, and of ourselves, with which we have not dared to come to terms. Someone who knew this was Franz Kafka. Kafka in 1903 was only 20 years old, and he was still some way from writing the novels and the stories—among them *The Trial, The Castle* and *The Metamorphosis*—which were to earn him a unique place in the history of the European imagination. But he already knew what was worth writing (and reading) and what wasn't. He sensed that a state of emergency would shortly be declared within the European psyche, and that a new kind of awareness would be needed to deal with it. The old order might seem to be intact in the Austro-Hungarian Empire of 1903, and the concept of the collective unconscious had not yet been formulated by C. G. Jung. But Kafka also sensed that someone would have to force that new kind of awareness upon us. Meanwhile, it was not the writer's first duty to help the reader to pass the time as agreeably as possible. "A book must be an ice axe," Kafka wrote to a friend, "to break the sea frozen within us." "If the book in our hands does not wake us, as with a fist that hammers on the skull, then it just isn't worth reading." That was the message.

Kafka and his ice axe could remind us of a German painting which, though not modern in date, is both a classic of clear-sightedness and the ancestor of much that is memorable in the art of the last hundred years: *The Frozen Sea* (fig. 1), which was painted by Caspar David Friedrich in 1822. This was a new kind of picture, with a new echo to it, and it is still the best image we have of the way in which human hopes and human ambitions can have the life crushed out of them by forces beyond our control. Friedrich took one of the vicissitudes of early Arctic exploration and turned it into a symbol of "history as nightmare." Such was the force of his emotional commitment, when allied to a steadfast and pellucid form of expression, that his private anxieties took on a universal and a timeless validity.

Like all the great symbols, *The Frozen Sea* will bear many interpretations and yield something new to all of them. It is a painting to which every age reacts in a different way. Friedrich never sold it. The sailing ship was for him, throughout his career, a symbol for all that was vulnerable and nerve-ridden in human affairs; but I believe that *The Frozen Sea* had a secret meaning for him, and one so poignant that he could not bear to part with the painting. It had an inner subject: the events of the immediate past in Germany. The disaster to which it refers is political as much as maritime. Friedrich was still the man who had painted, ten years earlier, a picture called *The Grave of One Who Fell for Freedom;* and when he painted *The Frozen Sea* he must have had in mind the Carlsbad Decrees of 1819, by which freedom of the press was abolished over a large part of Germany, political agitation was suppressed, the universities were brought under state control, and the free-spirited individual laid under suspicion of "conspiracy." That was "history as nightmare" in the 1820s. In how many countries is it not still with us?

Friedrich was the first major European artist to acknowledge the role in his work of the as-yet-unnamed unconscious. "Close your physical eye" was his advice to other painters. "Look first at your picture with the eye of the spirit, and bring to the light of day what you have seen in darkness." It is as if he knew, ahead

3

of his time, that the documentary, illustrative function would soon be wrested from art. Art had still the power, however, to come up with symbols so telling, so universal in their application, that they take rank among the experiences that orient us in life. One such was Goya's *The Colossus* (fig. 3). As much as anyone who ever lived, Goya carried within him the sense of history as nightmare. The offhand brutality of our own times is something to which Goya, in 19th-century Spain, gave definitive expression. Where he trod, it is pointless for other painters to follow; what has been done completely need not be done again. Goya had in an extreme degree the premonitory sense: he knew what kinds of behavior had come to stay. "No one," said Baudelaire of Goya, "has ventured further in the direction of the *possible* absurd." Now that the absurd is everywhere—in behavior so appalling that we have to give it an ironical name before we can bear to think about it all—we realize that to explore the "possible absurd" in such depth was as great a service to mankind as art can perform.

The Colossus gave us a new metaphor for nightmare. Just who the giant was, and just what he was doing, Goya left it to us to decide. He is an archetypal figure of dread; each generation gives him a new set of identity papers. To have some idea of the powers of art we have only to set *The Colossus* beside a comparable image from the 1930s: a still from *King Kong* (fig. 4). *King Kong* was a good movie, and the image reproduced here has entered into the folk-memory of our times. But beside the Goya how flat it is, how banal, how pedestrian! How much less terrifying is King Kong's petulant stance, with its conventional baring

4

of the teeth, than the total indifference of Goya's colossus, who does not even deign to look back at the scene of panic and terror beneath him!

Both *The Colossus* and *The Frozen Sea* stand for an important shift in the activities of the human imagination: the shift from allegory to symbol. Allegory in this context is the use of art to tell a story which is already familiar but cannot be told too often. Anyone who went to the Doges' Palace in Venice in the 1580s and was shown the new paintings by Veronese would immediately see that most of the paintings in question were about power, and about the fact that the Venetian Republic had power and intended to keep it. Allegory, in this instance, was doing its job well; Mars and Neptune were on the ceiling, and very fine they looked; but the implication was that Venetian power had the sanction of the gods and woe betide anyone who presumed to challenge it. Allegory had for centuries been one of the prime functions of art. Allegory in public places was confirmatory, by its very nature. If a painting was put up in church, or in the law courts, or in one of the seats of government, it was a safe bet that it would tell people that things were quite all right as they were. The painter was not going to say that religion was a hoax, or that the judges were ignorant and corrupt, or that the ruler was not fit to rule. When Tintoretto worked in the Doges' Palace, and Rubens worked for Marie de' Medici when she was Queen of France, and Tiepolo painted the great ceiling in the Bishop's Palace in Würzburg, they were being asked to uphold the status quo; and they did it, without demur. If they thought that the Doges had got above themselves, or that the Bishops were too free with the excellent local wine, they never said so.

By the 19th century the structure of obeisance, long shaken, fell apart. So did the structure of shared learning on which allegory could draw. The old confidence in society and its rulers, already undermined by the revolutions of the 18th century, was collapsing. ("Casca il mondo"—"The world is coming apart"— said the Papal Secretary of State in 1866, when the Prussians defeated the Austrians at the battle of Königgrätz.) Allegory in its great days depended on shared beliefs, and shared expectations, and allusions universally recognizable. But in the 19th century a new world was coming into being: a world in which many thoughtful people had not read Virgil and Ariosto, and didn't know one saint from another, and were convinced that the only thing in which they could believe completely was their own private emotional experience. Whole sections of humanity felt themselves orphaned. To accommodate all this—to express the poetry of dissent and the politics of disquiet—a new kind of art had to come into being.

3. Francisco Goya
The Colossus, c. 1808
Museo del Prado, Madrid

4. RKO Radio Pictures
King Kong, 1933
The Museum of Modern Art, New York
Film Stills Archive

5. Edouard Manet
Portrait of Stéphane Mallarmé, 1876
Musée du Louvre, Paris

6. Edvard Munch
Portrait of Stéphane Mallarmé,
  1896
Museum of Fine Arts, Boston

7. Paul Gauguin
Portrait of Stéphane Mallarmé, 1891
The Museum of Modern Art, New York

Mallarmé loved looking at pictures, and he loved the company of painters. That painters returned the compliment is clear from these three portraits—and above all from the Manet, which has just the easy, conversational note which is most often lacking in more formal portraiture.

SYMBOL AND AUTHORITY

Friedrich's had been a preindustrial sensibility: one that functioned in perfect unselfconsciousness before what now seems to us the second Fall of Man. By the 1880s the role of the imagination was in the ascendant, in that symbols alone could stand for thoughts too long repressed in made-to-order painting. Symbol was the free man's revenge upon authority. It was the essence of the symbol, in this context, that it did not tell a familiar story. In fact it didn't tell a story at all. It sowed a seed: of disquiet, wonder, speculation, doubt. It was an invaluable way of saying something very important without pinning oneself down. No tyrant was immune to the symbol; and the 1880s had their full share of tyrants and would-be tyrants. The time was approaching when James Joyce could say that "silence, exile and cunning" were the only conditions in which a major artist could go to work. The silence could be conditional, the exile a matter of inner adjustment, the cunning a strategy to keep out of authority's way. The essential was to keep the work intact. The symbol was the mine with which outdated ideas would be deftly blown sky high;

meanwhile, the vagrant imagination did better to shun company. It is significant that the life style of Symbolist painters like Gustave Moreau and Odilon Redon was private and obsessional, with none of the hearty, outgoing quality which had characterized Monet and Renoir in their youth.

But if the vagrant imagination did not have company in the Paris of the 1880s, it had backers. In poetry and painting alike, it was defended by masters of language: Stéphane Mallarmé, above all, and his fellow poets Jules Laforgue, Tristan Corbière and Jean Moréas. Symbolism is so much a matter of the individual imagination, and so little a matter of theory and doctrine, that groupings of this sort are valid primarily as a matter of historical convenience. Much of what is called Symbolist painting and poetry had nothing to do with "history as nightmare." It was, rather, a retreat into a dream world of epicene twitter and recondite allusions not worth disentangling. But many of the best poets agreed with many of the best painters that the dream was the essence of their activity, and that it should take priority at all

6

times. As for fidelity to the experience of everyday—other, lesser persons could take care of that. Painting and poetry were very close; already in 1864, 22 years before Jean Moréas wrote the "Symbolist Manifesto," Mallarmé was using the verb "to paint" when he defined his intentions in poetry.

Mallarmé, in matters of art, was fundamental not only to his own century but to ours as well. Whenever a work of art has a resonance that cannot be explained in literal terms, or in terms of information, Mallarmé is somewhere behind it. At the age of 22, he spoke of inventing a new use of language which would "paint not the thing itself but the effect that it produces." He was neither narrow nor doctrinaire in his tastes. A close friend of Manet, and the subject of what is perhaps the most elegant of all Manet's portraits, he wrote on Manet in the 1870s with an eloquence and an understanding which have not been surpassed. Artists of many persuasions loved him: when he died in 1898, Rodin, Renoir and Vuillard were among the people at his graveside.

He believed that straight description had no place in art. Of course it could teach, tell a specific story, link one fact to another. But the essential lay elsewhere: in the echo, the singular vibration, the symbol which could not be pinned down or explained away. "To *name* an object," Mallarmé wrote in 1891, "is to deprive the public of three-quarters of its pleasure. The identity of objects should be revealed gradually. Guesswork should enter into it. To *suggest*—that should be the poet's dream. In suggesting, he makes the best possible use of that mysterious thing, the symbol."

Mallarmé in writing this was out to break the domination of a tightly wrought, tightly metered poetry in which subject matter was precisely defined and images were drawn as if with an etching needle. But the distinction which he drew between naming and suggesting could apply just as much to the difference between painting which relies on what is given to the outward eye and painting which proceeds from an inner vision. Other poets underlined this difference. Tristan Corbière said, for instance, that "the only thing that the painter should paint is what he has never seen and never will see." Gustave Moreau, preeminent among painters of that sort, once said that he did not believe in what he could touch or in what he could see; the only things that he believed in were the things that he could *not* see.

Moreau was neither a bigot nor a doctrinaire, and in his last years he proved to be as inspiring and as liberal a teacher as France has ever produced. He had been close to Degas in his youth, but he never stooped to petty disparagement of painters whose practice differed from his own. Yet his work was anti-Impressionist by implication. In a period when nearly all the great

8. Gustave Moreau
Oedipus and the Sphinx, 1864
The Metropolitan Museum of Art, New York

10. Odilon Redon
Winged Head Flying over Sea, c. 1875
The Art Institute of Chicago

9. Odilon Redon
The Masque of the Red Death, 1883
The Museum of Modern Art, New York

It had for centuries been fundamental to French thought that the life of the mind was governed by reason and by logic. But in 1870 another point of view was put forward by Hippolyte Taine in his book on the intelligence. Of images he said: "The image, like the sensation it repeats, is by its very nature hallucinatory. Hallucination seems monstrous to us, but it is, on the contrary, the very fabric of our mental life." Redon's graphic work did not speak only for an isolated dreamer; it was a contribution to the natural history of the French intelligence.

paintings, from Courbet to Monet, had to do with the restatement of observable fact, Gustave Moreau kept open the line to an art of pure fantasy. In his own work he allowed his imagination to drive him to the very edge of incoherence, the very edge of self-revelation, the very edge of delirium. Despising what he

called "the sad accountancy of common sense," he offered himself as a living exemplar of its antithesis. For all the idiosyncrasy of his obsessions Moreau was right in there first, as Friedrich in other contexts had been right in there before him, with the obsessions of a later age. Moreau's *Oedipus* (fig. 8) is the archetypal fine-boned victim of a dilemma to which Freud gave universal status, just as Moreau's *Salome Dancing before Herod* (pl. I) prefigures Richard Strauss's treatment of the same subject in the opera first performed in 1905. Moreau for many years lived the life of a moneyed hermit—"a hermit," said Degas, "who knows the railroad schedules by heart"—but the frozen seas within him turned out, when melted, to set whole generations afloat.

Moreau was a favorite of the novelist J. K. Huysmans. Huysmans also saw the point of a younger artist, Odilon Redon, whose work he described in 1881 as "nightmare transposed into art"; and Redon did, in fact, pride himself on the idea. He thought that the Impressionists were the captives of their subject matter, that they could look at it from only one limited point of view, and that they were blind to anything that was not set down in front of their noses. Redon himself excelled in the epigrammatic form

11. Käthe Kollwitz
Riot (Plate 5 from *The Weavers* cycle), 1897
National Gallery of Art, Washington, D.C.

12. Hubert von Herkomer
On Strike, 1891
Royal Academy of Arts, London

of the black and white print; and it was in that form that he knew best how to welcome "the messenger of the unconscious, that most lofty and mysterious personage, who comes in her own good time. The vital thing," he went on, "is to submit to the unconscious. . . ."

Looking back at Moreau and Redon, with their admirably cut clothes, their ordered senior-citizens' lives and their circle of eminent friends and acquaintances, it seems paradoxical that they should stand with van Gogh, the outcast, and with Gauguin, the exile, in the Symbolist pantheon. But they were at one with Gauguin and van Gogh in believing that there should be more to art than is encompassed by everyday visual experience. Just what that "something more" might mean to us was put very well by Edvard Munch in 1889, when, as a man of 26, he defined the limitations of Impressionism once and for all: "I've had enough of 'interiors,' and 'people reading,' and 'women knitting.' I want to paint real live people who breathe, feel, suffer and live. People who see these pictures will understand that these are sacred matters, and they will take off their hats, as if they were in church."

Munch was not alone, of course, in wishing to create an art of concern. As we have seen, van Gogh was a born preacher.

Gauguin tried to take upon himself all the tribulations that western Europe was heir to. All over Europe, artists were aiming to enlarge the preoccupations of their well-to-do public. Some of them were convinced radicals like Käthe Kollwitz, who in 1897 produced a series of prints in homage to the Silesian weavers who had revolted against their masters in 1844 (fig. 11). Some of them were what Ibsen called "pillars of society." Hubert von Herkomer, for instance, was a great personage in late Victorian England, but in 1891 he surprised many of his admirers by sending to the Royal Academy a picture called *On Strike* (fig. 12), which was a gesture of solidarity toward the industrial poor.

These were honorable personal statements, and Käthe Kollwitz was, to the end of her long life (1867–1945), an outstandingly courageous and selfless individual. But she did not change the course of art: that role was reserved for Edvard Munch. Not only did he impose a new kind of sensibility in the 1890s, but he extended the idiom which van Gogh and Gauguin had made available. Munch had always made it his business to know what was going on in art, and when he was in Paris between 1889 and 1893 he looked about him hard and long and at what Rodin, in particular, was doing.

II. Odilon Redon
Roger and Angelica, c. 1910
The Museum of Modern Art, New York

Redon took the subject of this picture
from Ariosto's mock-epic poem *Orlando
Furioso.* To the right, chained stark
naked to a rock, is the hapless maiden
Angelica. Untold indignities would
come her way from a particularly
repellent sea-monster if it were not for
her rescuer, the knight Ruggiero (or
Roger), who can be seen on the left as
he speeds to her rescue on the back of
a fabled monster, half horse and half
eagle.

The same episode from Ariosto had
been painted by Ingres in 1819, and
Redon almost certainly knew the picture in question. Like Ingres, he was
fascinated by the subject of Roger and
Angelica and tried his hand at it more
than once. But, whereas Ingres reacted
with evident relish to the chance of
showing a beautiful woman in close-up
at a moment of acute agony, Redon
played down the sensational element in
the story in favor of intense, jewellike
color which gives the scene a dream-
like quality.

13. Auguste Rodin
Gates of Hell (detail, lower
  section of left door)
Philadelphia Museum of Art,
  Rodin Museum

THE GATES OF HELL—AND BEYOND

As a sculptor who aspired to work on the grandest scale and to become, in effect, the keeper of the public conscience, Rodin was bound to get into trouble. Sculpture makes people uneasy, to begin with, in a way that painting does not. A painting sits on the wall, and can be ignored. Most sculpture occupies the same space as ourselves, mimics our way of standing, and forces us to get out of its way. Sculpture which tells the truth about how we look is likely to offend against taboos so powerful, so deep-seated in our natures, that we are not even aware of their existence. But Rodin showed with his *Gates of Hell,* 1880–1917 (fig. 14), that he was not to be deflected by such considerations. The designation of "Symbolist" is quite inadequate to characterize the full range of Rodin's activity; but he was a true Symbolist insofar as he did not wish his imaginative subjects to have local, finite implications. "The imagination of the spectator," he once wrote, "should be given rein to roam at will. That is the role of art, as I see it: the form which it creates should furnish a pretext for the unlimited development of emotion."

That "unlimited development of emotion" was exactly what Munch had in mind when he studied the work of Rodin. In scale

14. Auguste Rodin
Gates of Hell, 1880–1917
Philadelphia Museum of Art, Rodin Museum

11

15. Auguste Rodin
The Earth, 1884
B. G. Cantor Art Foundation, Beverly Hills,
California

One of the most enigmatic of Rodin's single figures, and one which bears a particularly heavy load of symbolism, is *The Earth*. It is for each of us to decide whether the figure in question is raising itself from the primeval slime, as the first phase of man's long and checkered progress toward civilization, or whether it is sinking back, in defeat and despair.

and function, Rodin's *Gates of Hell* was intended to be the pessimist's counterpart to the great affirmations of faith which had been among the highest achievements of European art for more than fifteen hundred years. Unlike the monumental sculptured doors of Santa Sabina in Rome, San Zeno in Verona and San Lorenzo in Florence, these gates were to bring no consolation to those who passed beneath the lintel. Rodin's message was, on the contrary, that (as Albert Elsen has said in his book on Rodin) mankind was "adrift in an empire of night; separated from, rather than being the victim of, its deity; born with a fatal duality of desire and an incapability to fulfill it; damned on both sides of the tomb to an internal Hell of passions."

A discouraging point of view, decidedly; but one not easily refuted. Humanity was in a bad way as it trundled toward the year 1914. The conditions of life in industrial society were such as to sunder man from man, condemning each and all to an ever-greater alienation. Rodin did not plan his huge scheme in advance but proceeded according to the imperatives of the uncon-

scious. As he saw it, humanity had no sooner raised itself from the primeval slime than it gave in, unprotesting, to the tyranny of Self; his myriad figures, twisting and turning in limbo, are emblems of the disconnectedness of modern life.

Munch learned from Rodin how to release the innate expressiveness of the human body. And although Rodin was 23 years his senior, Munch was enough a man of the 19th century to aspire to make a complete panorama—a three-volume novel in paint—of the human condition. He was to get the chance more than once; but meanwhile he displayed certain gifts which we are likely to underestimate now that we have so long taken his pictures for granted. He showed that easel painting was still very much alive at a time when the going thing in Paris, with Bonnard, with Vuillard and with their friends, was the big wall decoration. And he showed how to paint Symbolist pictures in which the human body, every bit of it, was as expressive as the body of a great actor on stage.

Munch also had a playwright's sense of economy. Nothing is in his pictures that does not need to be there. And what is there has in the highest degree, even today, the power to disturb and disquiet. Like Friedrich in *The Frozen Sea*, Munch drew on his own circumstances: the fact, for example, that his mother and his sister both died of tuberculosis while he was still a schoolboy. Like Moreau, he allowed his feelings about women to color his work from start to finish. He was not quite so frank as Moreau, who said in an unguarded moment that he found the iniquities of his Salome "not in the subject itself, but in the quintessence of womankind as I see it in life—woman, with her craving for unhealthy emotions and her stupidity, which is so intense that she does not grasp the horror of even the most dreadful situations." Munch would never have said that, but then he had acted out his beliefs more directly in his work. Nowhere do we find more vividly portrayed the late 19th-century's belief in woman-as-sorceress. We come across that belief in the novel, in the drama, in poetry, in the opera house, in the two words *femme fatale*. In this, as in so much else, Baudelaire was a pioneer: his *Les Fleurs du Mal* (1857) is stamped on almost every page with the idea of female seduction as something elemental, a force of nature not to be turned aside, much less resisted. That same idea comes out in the character of Kundry in Wagner's *Parsifal* (1882); it permeates the action of Dostoevsky's *The Idiot* (1869) in the character of Nastasia Petrovna; and if it was difficult at that time to be quite so candid in the legitimate theater, there were redoubtable instances of woman-as-willpower in the Scandinavian drama. Who can forget Hedda Gabler burning the manuscript of her former lover's lifework, in Ibsen's play, or the central figure in

16. Edvard Munch
Program cover: *Solveig and Mother Aase,* 1896
The Brooklyn Museum, New York

17. Edvard Munch
Woman, 1895
The Museum of Modern Art, New York

18. Edvard Munch
Ashes, 1894
Nasjonalgalleriet, Oslo

19. Edvard Munch
Jealousy, 1896
The Museum of Modern Art, New York

13

III. Edvard Munch
The Voice, 1893
Museum of Fine Arts, Boston

IV. Edvard Munch
The Dance of Life, 1899–1900
Nasjonalgalleriet, Oslo

For the greater part of his life Munch was preoccupied with the idea of painting a series of pictures which, when put together, would constitute a complete panorama of human life. He completed a modest version of it for the foyer of a theater in Berlin. Later, in 1922, he tried to compress the idea into a series of 12 paintings for a chocolate factory in Oslo; and sometimes there were single paintings which, like *The Dance of Life,* tried to show the whole gamut of human existence at once. Munch felt so strongly and so deeply for this subject that he was ready to adopt a system of cues which another artist would have rejected as too banal: as here, for instance, where the white dress of the girl on the left stands for an as yet unblemished purity, the black dress and tortured demeanor of the woman on the right stand for mourning and rejection, and the red dress of the woman in the middle stands for a delight in the passing moment. In the background, to left and to right, goatish couples symbolize the baser life. As always, it is the solitary figures who most engage Munch's sympathy.

20. Edvard Munch
Military Band on the Karl Johann Street, 1889
Kunsthaus, Zürich

21. Edvard Munch
Little Girls in Aasgaardstrand, 1904–05
Munch-museet, Oslo

Strindberg's *The Father,* consigned to a straitjacket by his womenfolk? We still find all this strong meat when we encounter it; but Munch had experienced it in life, and he relived it in his work.

Munch's emotional experience was of the kind which can be made bearable only if it is transformed by art. Munch's mother died when he was five. His father turned to the church for consolation and became a prey to religious anxieties which unfitted him for the ordinary traffic of life. (Munch said later that "disease and insanity were the black angels at my cradle.") As a grown man, Munch had great charm, a noble bearing and good looks of a statuesque sort which he retained even into old age. But these endowments did not save him from the most lurid and melodramatic of private entanglements. When he was 40, for instance, he was involved with a girl who had herself laid out, as if on her deathbed, in an attempt to prevent him from leaving her; and when she threatened to shoot herself and Munch tried to restrain her, the gun went off accidentally and he lost one of his fingers in the struggle. Two or three years later he had to leave Norway after a public brawl with another man. As late as the 1930s Munch was still reliving that day in his work—still picturing the look of his bloodied antagonist as he staggered along the narrow lane toward Munch's house, and still picturing the reflex of instinct with which he himself had picked up a gun as if to ward off a second attack.

Munch was able to share these experiences with us in a way that is neither garrulous nor self-pitying. He was also able to give them a universal implication. (A later painter, Oskar Kokoschka, said that Munch had been the first man to enter "the modern Inferno" and come back to tell how it was.) Art was for Munch what the theater was for Strindberg: "a *Biblia pauperum,* or Bible in pictures." He could have said, with Strindberg, that he "found 'the joy of life' in life's cruel and mighty conflicts"—and in the colossal discharges of psychic energy to which they gave rise. In dealing with those "cruel and mighty conflicts," Munch undressed feelings the way bodies are undressed in the act of love.

All this is made clear in such classic Munch subjects as *The Death-Chamber, Jealousy* (fig. 19) and *The Dance of Life* (pl. IV). In a painting like the *Virginia Creeper* of 1898 (pl. V), Munch uses a perfectly ordinary aspect of suburban horticulture to make us feel that the whole of Nature is hemorrhaging in sympathy with the tormented man in the foreground. Munch came from a part of the world in which Nature often seems to side with the extremes of human feeling; and Nature in his paintings is neither indifferent nor hostile. She figures, rather, as the accomplice of mankind and as a commentator who gives a new amplitude (and

22. Edvard Munch
Anxiety, 1896
The Museum of Modern
Art, New York

23. Ernst Ludwig Kirchner
Portrait of Erich Heckel,
1908
Städtisches Karl-Ernst-
Osthaus-Museum,
Hagen, Germany

what Rodin had called "an unlimited development") to emotions which in life are often repressed.

It is a part of the genius of Munch that he brings us face to face with aspects of life which we would otherwise neglect or ignore. If he shows a crowd streaming toward us along a city street, we sense that the crowd could at any moment be gunned down. If he paints a group of uncorrupted young girls—and no one was ever better at doing this—we see them as hostages on whom life will make heavy demands, sooner rather than later. If he paints a portrait, there is something peculiarly moving about his frank, open, frontal approach: we feel that this is how it should be, but so rarely is, when one human being confronts another. Munch gives us an object lesson in the use of color and in the nature of composition; but, more than that, he teaches us to live with our own experience and not be afraid of it.

GERMANY REINVENTED

If someone were to say "Munch" when asked to guess the authorship of the two paintings shown in figure 23 and plate VI, he would not be so far wrong as to have made a fool of himself. Neither painting could have been painted without Munch's example. The *Portrait of Erich Heckel* (1908) has precisely the tall thin format, the open and unambiguous stance before life, and the peremptory outlining of the figure against a light background which we associate with Munch's portraits of men. The Dresden *Street* (1907) has, again, many traits which are characteristic of Munch. It is in that same way that Munch sets his figures to face

V. Edvard Munch
Virginia Creeper, 1898
Munch-museet, Oslo

18

VI. Ernst Ludwig Kirchner
Street, Dresden, 1907
The Museum of Modern Art, New York

24. Erich Heckel
The Village Dance, 1908
Nationalgalerie, Berlin

25. Erich Heckel
Walkers by the Grunewaldsee, 1911
Museum Folkwang, Essen

the observer—as they might face a firing squad, head-on; his, equally, is the way of allowing a blank space to ooze and eddy its way upward from the bottom of the canvas. Munch had no equal when it came to handling metropolitan crowds. Where the Impressionists rendered the Parisian crowd in terms of petals and dabs and commas of pure color, Munch put real people, complete, on the canvas.

In point of fact, these pictures are by Ernst Ludwig Kirchner. Kirchner was 16 years younger than Munch, but he had in common with him the feeling that too much of life was being left out of art. When he was 20 years old, he was appalled by what then passed for "modern German painting." "The content of those pictures, and their execution, were as depressing as the public's total lack of interest," he wrote later. "Inside the gallery there were those pale, lifeless daubs. Outside, there was the flood of life itself, with its color, its sunshine, its sadness. . . . Why didn't those worthy gentlemen paint real life? Because it moves, that's why. They neither see it nor understand it. And then I thought—why shouldn't I try? And so I did."

The intention was not far from Munch's. But the environment, the social situation, the climate of belief—all these were quite different. Munch and the friends of his youth had axed their way through the frozen seas of Scandinavian provincialism, and very few people in Scandinavia had thanked them for it. Munch himself did much of his best work in exile; some of his writer friends were sent to jail for novels now forgotten but vital at the time; Ibsen had a very long haul before he became, in old age, a national hero.

Germany between 1900 and 1914 was not at all like that. But it had problems of its own. It had, for instance, an absolute ruler, in the person of Kaiser Wilhelm II, who had fixed ideas about modern art. "Art is not art," he said in a speech in 1901, "if it transgresses the laws and barriers laid down by Me. The word 'liberty' is often misused and can lead to license and presumption. . . . Art should make it possible for the lower echelons of society to raise themselves to the ideals which the German people is now alone in possessing. Art which merely portrays misery is a sin against the German people. . . ." This is the context in

26. Erich Heckel
Two Men by a Table (a scene from Dostoevsky's
   The Idiot), 1912
Hamburger Kunsthalle, Hamburg

Dostoevsky's books were still a novelty in German translation
when Heckel painted this picture, which is an unacknowledged
rendering of the climactic scene in Dostoevsky's *The Idiot*, when
Mishkin and Rogozhin talk in secret beneath a reproduction of
Holbein's *Dead Christ*. The exact nature of the Expressionist vision
could hardly be better summarized than in the taut, nerve-ridden,
elongated figures of the two men and the subtly distorted
perspective of the room.

which we should view such classics of their kind and date as
Menzel's *The Departure of Kaiser Wilhelm from Berlin on July
31, 1870, to Join the Troops at the Front* (Volume 1).

But they did find their way, even so, into German painting, and
at just the time (1905–09) when Richard Strauss in *Salome* and
Elektra was changing the whole notion of what could, and what
could not, be done in the opera house. Both works were first
heard in Dresden; and it was in Dresden that Kirchner and his
friends Erich Heckel and Karl Schmidt-Rottluff invented, between
1905 and 1911, a new kind of German art. Dresden before 1914
was not at all provincial in the sense that Oslo was provincial in
Munch's early days. It had a first-rate theater and a first-rate opera
house, a waterfront on the Elbe which was one of the most beautiful sights in Europe, and Old Master collections which were
worth crossing the world to see. It had dealers' galleries which
were particularly active and discerning. Anyone who lived in
Dresden between 1896 and 1906 could see the work of Monet,
Cézanne, Munch, Seurat, Gauguin and van Gogh not in ones and
twos but in bulk; and what they did not see would be filled out

by the art magazines which in Dresden, as elsewhere, were the
accepted currency of the new: *Jugend, Pan, The Studio,* and
Insel.

To exactly what extent Kirchner and his friends were influ-
enced by the European art of the immediate past is not our main
concern—perhaps luckily, since they never welcomed inquiries
on this subject and were likely to deny that they owed anything
at all to Munch or to Matisse, whose work Kirchner saw when he
was in Berlin in January, 1909. What we have to examine here is,
rather, the extent to which they brought to German art the new
kind of awareness which Kafka had posited in 1903. Did they
awaken their contemporaries "as with a fist hammering on the
skull"? And if so, how?

Their life style offers an initial clue. Instead of a conventional
studio in an "artist's quarter," they began by renting an empty
butcher's shop in a working-class suburb. Dresden had a very
well-equipped school of art, but Kirchner, Bleyl, Heckel and
Schmidt-Rottluff were students of architecture, not of art, and
they never changed over. When they banded together as a group

27. Ernst Ludwig Kirchner
Woman Buttoning Her Shoe, 1913 (?)
The Museum of Modern Art, New York

28. Ernst Ludwig Kirchner
The Blue House in the Potholder District, 1909
The Museum of Modern Art, New York

and called themselves "Die Brücke" (The Bridge), they did not address themselves to an established middle class. Their first exhibitions (October and December, 1906) were held in a lamp factory in the suburban working-class district of Dresden-Löbtau. There were conventions in the Germany of that time as to how an artist's studio should look; but visitors to the former butcher's shop (to which was later added a former shoe shop in the same neighborhood) were met by a way of life which was a deliberate affront to "good society": floors piled high with cigarette butts, naked girls ambling to and fro, subversive conversation at every hour of the day, almost nothing but cake to eat and the risk at

every moment of an impromptu reading from Nietzsche or Walt Whitman. A particular favorite was Whitman's "We Two Boys Together Clinging"; and one may doubt if Kaiser Wilhelm would have approved its last three lines:

Misers, menials, priests alarming, air breathing,
water drinking, on the turf or sea-beach dancing,
Cities wrenching, ease scorning, statutes mocking,
feebleness chasing,
Fulfilling our foray.

Kirchner and his friends took a long time to find what we now call "the Brücke style": so long, in fact, that Kirchner in later life tried to conceal the fact by back-dating certain of his pictures. It mattered to him that he should have begun to use flat, strong color contrasts only after the French Fauve painters had been seen in Dresden in 1908; but it doesn't matter so much to us, because we are more interested in the specifically German aspect of the Brücke—the way, in other words, in which they made themselves felt through the great eiderdown of German complacency before 1914.

That complacency was a late manifestation of 19th-century *Gemütlichkeit:* a quality defined by the literary historian J. P.

VII. Karl Schmidt-Rottluff
Houses at Night, 1912
The Museum of Modern Art, New York

Schmidt-Rottluff had come to Dresden as an architectural student in 1905. It was he who gave the Brücke group its name, and it was he who invited Nolde to join the Brücke in 1906. Not long before 1914 Edvard Munch, after looking at some black and white prints by Schmidt-Rottluff, spent a sleepless night; on coming down to breakfast he said "May God protect us! Evil times are coming." The sense of nightmare persists, equally, in this vision of a deserted street.

29. (far left) Hans Baldung (called Grien)
The Temptation of Eve
The National Gallery of Canada, Ottawa

30. (left) Anonymous
Shawm Player, 1380
Germanisches Nationalmuseum, Nuremberg

In early German art there can be found both a particular stylized physical type and a distinctive emotional atmosphere. Kirchner and his friends were as attentive to one as to the other.

Stern as "a curious and unique configuration of time-honored habits, rich meals, ancient or at least old-fashioned furniture, solid broadcloth and solid moral maxims. . . ." Property and propriety were conjoined in *Gemütlichkeit;* between them, they smothered the free spirit. Just occasionally that spirit revenged itself: in a novel by Wilhelm Carl Raabe, for instance, called *Documents of the Vogelsang District* (1896). Nothing else in contemporary German literature quite equaled the climactic scene in Raabe's novel, where the main character comes back to his native town after making a success of life elsewhere. He has money, he has a house that has been in his family for generations, and within that house he has all the apparatus of *Gemütlichkeit:* a veritable German ark filled with furniture, linen, carpets, heavy curtains, bibelots of every kind. He waits for winter; and when winter comes he steadily and consistently, day after day, burns

all his belongings. *"Er heizte mit seinem Hausrat,"* says Raabe, in a five-word sentence that denied the materialistic basis of German life: "He burned his belongings to keep warm."

Kirchner had something of that sort in mind. To achieve it, he springboarded backward in time to the days when German art meant Dürer and Cranach and to the still earlier days when German architecture meant the lean, arrowy forms of German Gothic. He had seen that German Impressionism was fundamentally a compromise rather than a bold break with the art preceding it: greasy in physical terms, it was greasy also in its social attitudes. Kirchner and his friends looked elsewhere for their ideal Germany. Looking at Hans Baldung's *The Temptation of Eve* (fig. 29), or at the bronze figure of Hansel the shawm player, which was made in Nuremberg in the 1380s (fig. 30), we see that ideal made visible. Kirchner saw the Brücke group as *Neu-*

24

31. Ernst Ludwig Kirchner
Panama Girls, 1910 (?)
North Carolina Museum of Art, Raleigh

deutsche: "new Germans." "German creativity is fundamentally different from Latin creativity," he wrote. "The Latin takes his forms from the object as it exists in nature. The German creates his form from fantasy, from an inner vision peculiar to himself. The forms of visible nature serve him as symbols only . . . and he seeks beauty not in appearance but in something beyond."

By "symbol," here, Kirchner did not mean the delicate vibration which Mallarmé had had in mind. He meant something robust, forthright, provocative. His idea of a symbol was something that said "Live more naturally! It's a mistake not to." Living more naturally meant breaking with the current notion of fine art and relying, for example, on the antithesis of the woodcut, the primeval clash of plain black against plain white, as against the curdled sauces of German Impressionism. It meant using color contrasts that looked both caustic and gaudy when set against the super-civilized procedures of Matisse. The human beings in Brücke paintings often looked as if they had been carved out of

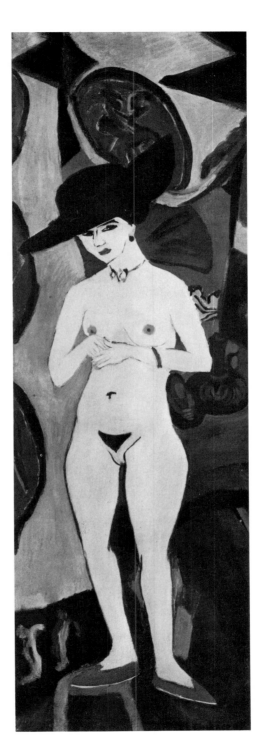

32. Ernst Ludwig Kirchner
Standing Nude with Hat,
1910–20
Städtische Galerie,
Frankfurt

25

VIII. Ernst Ludwig Kirchner
Street, Berlin, 1913
The Museum of Modern Art, New York

33. Ernst Ludwig Kirchner
Wrestlers in a Circus, c. 1906–09
The Cleveland Museum of Art

wood with a rather blunt knife; and when the Brücke portrayed big-city life it was rarely without a hint of underlying menace in the portrayal.

All this they did in the name of an undefined but ever-present emergency. History as nightmare presides over just about all the best work of the Brücke group. Sometimes they simply showed an intelligent awareness of what was going on around them: the sexual candor of Wedekind's play *Pandora's Box* (1904) has obvious echoes in their work, as did the first complete publication (from 1907 onward) of Dostoevsky in German translation. But fundamentally the vision of the world which they had to offer

was peculiar to themselves, despite its borrowing from the German past, from African and Indian art, and from Munch and Matisse. It is a vision in which the individual is battered about by society and thereafter left to fend for himself.

Kirchner had been a compulsive draftsman from childhood onward; and when he came to paint his big Dresden street scene, he had no difficulty in finding a graphic equivalent for the quirks of character and deportment which he had been studying for the greater part of his life. He had never drawn "from the model," in the academic sense; what he drew, he had lived. The Dresden *Street* is, on one level, almost dandified in its use of the

34. Ernst Ludwig Kirchner
Nude Dancers, 1909
The Museum of Modern Art, New York

continually varied hat shapes, back and forth across the upper half of the canvas. Kirchner is no less ingenious in his animation of the shallower space on the right-hand side of the picture; how subtly does he suggest that these are people possessed by the city! Yet the picture is neither decorative nor polemical; the drawing sees to that. Each person is an individual, an identifiable Dresdener hurrying to keep up. If we ask "To keep up with *what?*"—history has an answer.

After six years of collective activity in Dresden, the Brücke moved to Berlin in the fall of 1911. It was a fateful change. Dresden by comparison with Berlin was still slow-moving, almost countrified; Berlin had a rapacious, uncaring, over-energized quality. 1912 was, whether coincidentally or not, the year in which Kirchner "came out" in international terms. He met Franz Marc and was made welcome in the Blaue Reiter, the Munich group formed by Marc and Kandinsky. He met Munch at an international art exhibition in Cologne. He was invited to take part in the Armory Show in New York, Chicago and Boston. Above all, he developed a new way of handling the metropolitan scene.

In the Berlin *Street* of 1913 (pl. VIII), we find ourselves in the world of pure Expressionism. Bodies are elongated beyond the possibilities of anatomy; color bears no relation to the colors of every day; distortions take us into the realms of hallucination. This is the Berlin which the Expressionist cinema was to evoke a

decade later. (It was an Expressionist painter, Ludwig Meidner, who designed the sets in 1923 for one of the most nightmarish of early German films, *The Street.*)

It should be said that the real Berlin was not at all like this. It had been developed in the second half of the 19th century in terms of broad avenues and generous intersections, with sidewalks wide enough for the most elaborate of sexual maneuvering and really very little that resembled the slotlike streets and converging skylines of Expressionist painting. Kirchner tackled this real Berlin quite straightforwardly in daytime suburban townscapes; but when the night-prowlers went through the routines of appraisal in midtown Berlin, Kirchner presented them as hemmed in by their environment, with barely enough room for one silk-lined marauder to squeeze past another. A long, thin, constantly repeated daggerlike formal motif runs throughout the Berlin *Street;* only the antediluvian taxi is exempt from it. There is, once again, a foretaste of the Expressionist cinema in Kirchner's drastic way with perspective: the sidewalk, for instance, rears up behind the promenaders as if it was about to throw them forward and out of the picture altogether. It is as if the emergency were too great to allow of a third dimension. This is a scene of predation, in which human beings are stalked by other human beings and a hard bargain may soon be struck. Kirchner intensified its effect by using color in a way which was quite new for him. In Dresden he had worked primarily with forthright oppositions of complementary color. In the Berlin *Street* he worked with colors that were adjacent to one another on the color wheel: neighbor was set against neighbor. As Dr. Donald E. Gordon, in his book on Kirchner, puts it: "The interplay is between the rich dark blues of the central figures and the intense colors of the sidewalk; though ranging from crimson to cerise, they are dominated by an acrid scarlet. The purple robe of the nearest figure (whose hair is red) is the necessary median to these adjacent hues."

The painters of the Brücke epitomized also that particular roughness of expression which has characterized a great deal of radical art in this century. What they had to say was too urgent to be tidied up. If the finished canvas looked like a relief map of the painter's agitation, so much the better: gentility was out. What mattered was truth to the moment and to the unfettered play of instinct. Humanity had arrived at one of the hinge-points of history, and it was the duty of the painter to bear witness as best he could. This might seem to rule out—and in the case of Kirchner and his friends it did rule out—those grand panoramic adventures which had always been the supreme ambition of the allegorical painter.

KLIMT AND THE SEVERED HEAD

Adventures of that kind were not likely to come the way of radical painters in Germany while Kaiser Wilhelm II was on the throne; but they did come the way of Munch, who spent some of the best years of his life (1909–14) on mural paintings—some of them as much as 38 feet in length—for Oslo University. And a comparable opportunity was given in Vienna to Gustav Klimt when, in October, 1894, he was invited to paint three large panels—*Jurisprudence, Medicine* (fig. 37) and *Philosophy* (fig. 36)—for the great hall or Aula of the University of Vienna. It must have seemed quite a safe choice; Klimt was known as a reliable young man who could work to order. He was practiced, docile, meticulous, and he turned in his work on time. There was every reason to suppose that his work for the University would go through without incident.

Klimt was, moreover, in human terms the exact opposite of almost all the artists with whom we have lately dealt. Easy and convivial by nature, Klimt was accepted throughout his life as a man who did honor to his generation: not for him the subterranean political motivation and the eventual exile of Goya. He strode into life as a champion swimmer strides into the sea. Of course such looks can be deceptive, and Klimt, in point of fact, had his full share of inner anxieties; but these never compared with the alienation of Munch, who in 1908–09 was restored to mental stability only after eight months of intensive care in a clinic, or with the slow decline of Kirchner, who died by his own hand in Switzerland in 1938 after a long period in exile. The crippled emotional life of the mother-bound Moreau was at a far extreme from the royal freedom with which Klimt appeared to move from one attachment to another. Klimt was at one with the world.

Or was he? It did not seem so when the first of the three panels, *Philosophy,* was put on view in 1900. *Medicine* was shown in 1901; and in 1903 all three were shown together, though *Jurisprudence* was still not finished. There was in every case a most terrible uproar—so much so that in the fall of 1903 the contract was annulled. The three paintings were never installed in the University; and, as they were destroyed in a fire during the last phase of World War II, we can judge them only by the old and imperfect photographs which have survived and by a few working drawings in Viennese public collections. It is clear from these, however, that Klimt did not represent philosophy, jurisprudence and medicine in terms of superior wisdom, or of an intellectual majesty that stood high above the battle, or of a long view that put all our earthly concerns in perspective. The imagery in general was nearer, if anything, to that of Rodin's *Gates of Hell.* What

35. Emil Nolde
Solomon and His Wives, 1911
The Museum of Modern Art, New York

Emil Nolde was considerably older than the founder-members of the Brücke group, but at their invitation he formed a loose alliance with them in 1906–07 and spent much of his time in Dresden. His graphic work soon showed (as here) both the benefits which he had derived from his Brücke friends and a robust, single-minded identification with his subject matter. Nolde's was too powerful a nature to remain part of a team for long, and after 18 months he decided to go his own solitary way.

had philosophy to do with families twirling in limbo? Or medicine with an over-decorated temptress who was feeding her pet snake from a glass saucer? Or jurisprudence with the seductive young women, dressed only in their superabundant hair, who

29

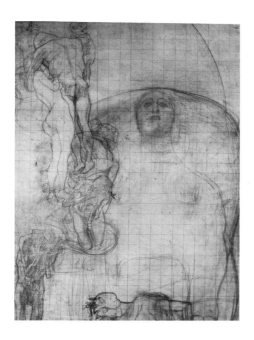

36. Gustav Klimt
Study for "Philosophy,"
1898–99
Historisches Museum der
Stadt, Vienna

37. Gustav Klimt
Study for "Medicine," 1901
Graphische Sammlung
Albertina, Vienna

fixed the spectator with looks that were anything but judicial? It was all too much for the Ministerial committees, and too much for the outraged faculty members within the University, and too much for the general public.

Klimt had, of course, changed a great deal since the contract came his way. In 1892 he had lost both his father, an engraver by profession, and his younger brother Ernst, who had worked with him on more than one laborious decoration. In ways not yet disentangled, these misfortunes seem to have liberated Klimt; after several years' silence he emerged in 1898 as an artist of a completely different kind and a vastly greater stature. The docile journeyman-decorator became the spokesman of his age—or, more exactly, of that age's unconscious longings and fears. In the Vienna of Gustav Mahler, Arnold Schoenberg and Sigmund Freud, Gustav Klimt was a person of consequence. He was present at table on the occasion when Mahler first set eyes on his future wife, and he was one of the very few people who saw Mahler constantly after his marriage. When the younger Viennese artists formed the Vienna Secession in 1897, Klimt was the natural choice for their first president. The amenable tradesman of the early 1890s had turned by 1900 into a poet who could take a look at the worst and come back and say how it was. This is what Klimt did in his three panels for the University: what if medicine and philosophy and jurisprudence had no effect what-

ever on the conditions of human life? What if medicine could not heal our deepest ills, and jurisprudence had nothing to do with justice, and philosophy could not assuage the inner torments of mankind? Klimt in 1893 had gone along with society in its every detail. By 1900 he had brought that same society face to face with itself. People did not like it, any more than they liked it when Mahler presented them, in work after work, with a fragmented and deeply pessimistic account of one man's passage through life.

The University panels are by no means Klimt's only claim upon us. His position in art history, and in the history of human inclinations, is owed quite as much to his easel paintings as to the three panels which were left to burn by the German SS troops as they withdrew from Austria in 1945. Klimt's mature style was, on one level, a most dexterous amalgam of ingredients from the international style in European decoration at the turn of the century. He took from the decorative paintings of an Englishman, Edward Burne-Jones. He took from the work of a Scottish architect and designer, Charles Rennie Mackintosh, and from the work of Mrs. Mackintosh, the painter Margaret Macdonald. He knew all about the twining and twirling of linear decoration as it was practiced by the artists of Art Nouveau in Germany, in Belgium and in France. He had had on his doorstep in 1898 a survey of the international style at the Vienna Secession. Like most Central Euro-

IX. Gustav Klimt
Judith I, 1901
Österreichische Galerie, Vienna

Vienna has always had more than its quota of beautiful women, but in the period before 1914 they had a particular bloom and a specific poise. They also had a fullness of nature, a psychological complexity, which found the amplest possible outlet in action. Klimt's *Judith* is pure Viennese in physical type. She could be on her way to a costume-ball, except for one thing: we have no doubt that the severed head which she holds is a real one, and that she has been to bed for many nights and of set purpose with a Babylonian general, and that it was her hand that wielded the knife.

   Klimt does not set himself up as judge, in such cases. He is at the farthest possible remove from Aubrey Beardsley, who chose the subject of Salome because it allowed him to make public his fear and loathing of women. Klimt simply took it for granted that men and women have their way with one another and that from time to time, whether literally or in metaphor, heads roll.

38. Charles Rennie Mackintosh
The Scottish Musical Review, 1896
The Museum of Modern Art, New York

39. *(far right)* Frank Lloyd Wright
Windows (3)
The Metropolitan Museum of Art, New York

In the 1890s the overriding influence of
Art Nouveau, in both Europe and America,
could not help but be reflected in art.
Gustav Klimt in Vienna was part of an international or intercontinental movement
of taste, perfectly exemplified in this poster
by **Charles Rennie Mackintosh** for *The
Scottish Musical Review.*
  The famous whiplash curves gradually
straightened out as the new century
progressed; yet the Frank Lloyd Wright
window (done for the playhouse of the
Coonley House, Riverside, Illinois, built in
1912) still retains the sensibilities of the
style. An architect here has the last word
on a movement originally begun by
architects.

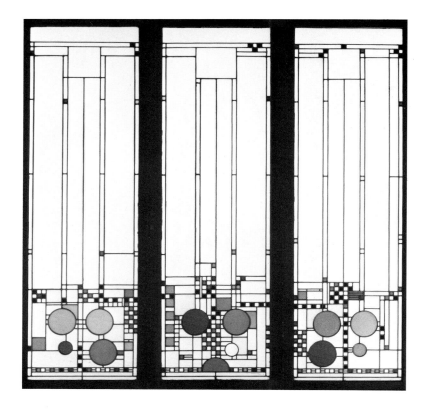

peans of his generation, he had looked at the work of Aubrey
Beardsley; and he knew that there was something of a renaissance in the applied arts, and that that renaissance had made use
of gold and silver and enamel and precious stones in a way that
looked quite new.

He could have known all this and been no more than a low-
powered eclectic: a provincial pirate, quick to sight the spoils but
too weak to bring more than a part of them home. But in point
of fact Klimt's easel pictures are unlike anyone else's. Not many
of them survive, and they are not easy to see. But they have claims
upon us which are unique. Nobody, to begin with, has given us
so complete a portrait of a certain kind of European womanhood
at its apogee.

Klimt was without equal, in my view, when it came to portray-
ing women whom he admired and respected. Perhaps his closest
friend was his sister-in-law Emilie Flöge, one of a trio of liberated
young Viennese women who ran a successful dress shop in
Vienna at a time when young ladies of good family were not ex-
pected to go into trade. Klimt could never see too much of her,

and when he was brought home in January, 1918, after the stroke
which was to kill him, his first words were, "Get Emilie here."
Not surprisingly, the portrait of her which he painted in 1902
(pl. X) is a masterpiece of delicate insight. It is also remarkable for
the amount of flat patterning of a purely ornamental sort which
Klimt managed to combine with the naturalistic modeling of the
head. Not only did Klimt love densely patterned materials for
their own sake, but he was sufficiently a man of his own time to
think hard and often about the extent to which the canvas should
be presented quite straightforwardly as "a flat surface covered
with colors assembled in a certain order." As he grew older, that
flat surface played an ever greater role in his paintings; the human body was portrayed, as always, with a most delectable im-
mediacy, but it was set more and more in a jeweled surround
that paid no regard whatsoever to plausibility. If that surround
could be read in terms of jewelry, or of a wall-hanging, or of a
dress elaborated beyond the dreams of even the best designer in
Vienna, so much the better. If it couldn't, Klimt didn't care; people must find their way about the picture as best they could.

32

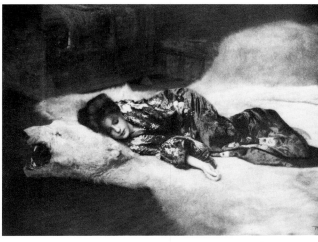

40. (*left*) Rudolf Eickemeyer, Jr.
"In My Studio" (Photograph of Evelyn Nesbit
   on a bearskin rug), 1901
Hudson River Museum, Yonkers, N.Y.

The ideal of feminine beauty to which Klimt gave supreme expression
was to be found in other countries, and in other media, in the first
years of the century. The words *femme fatale* sum it up; and
Eickemeyer, like Klimt, knew where to find it.

41. (*bottom left*) Gustav Klimt
Danaë, 1907–08
Private collection, Graz, Austria

42. (*bottom right*) Gustav Klimt
Portrait of Margaret Stonborough-Wittgenstein, 1905
Neue Pinakothek, Munich

X. Gustav Klimt
Portrait of Emilie Flöge, 1902
Historisches Museum der Stadt, Vienna

XI. Gustav Klimt
Water Serpents I, 1904–07
Österreichische Galerie, Vienna

It seems probable that Klimt got the idea for his water nymphs from a wall
decoration, which he could have seen in Vienna, by the Scottish architect and
designer Charles Rennie Mackintosh and his wife Margaret Macdonald. This
in its turn was based on a poem by Maurice Maeterlinck, then one of the most
famous writers in Europe. But Klimt gave the subject a heightened emotional
charge and overtones of an outlawed passion; of the gentility of English Art
Nouveau, no trace remains.

43. Oskar Kokoschka
Cover design for *Der Sturm*, July 14, 1910
Private collection, London

Insofar as modern art had to win converts among the Central European public before 1914, much of the work was done by periodicals like *Der Sturm*, edited from 1910 onward by the art dealer, publisher and cultural impresario Herwarth Walden. This particular issue carried the text of a play called *Murder, Hope of Women* (a title which bespeaks the whole Expressionist era) by the young Austrian painter Oskar Kokoschka; Kokoschka also made a characteristically arresting drawing for the cover.

44. Ludwig Meidner
Apocalyptic Mood, 1913
The St. Louis Art Museum

45. (*opposite page*) Max Klinger
The Glove, No. 9: "The Rape," 1878–80
The Museum of Modern Art, New York

A plate from *The Glove* series of etchings by German Symbolist Max Klinger, who studied for a while under Böcklin (fig. 47). Depicting, with superior draftsmanship, the peculiar tale of a woman's lost glove and the strange and perilous adventures which befall it, the series is a rarefied piece of Symbolist art.

Sometimes the ornamentation was vivid but sparse, and placed with a Whistlerian delicacy. Sometimes it was made an effect of overpowering luxury; the observer might well have been reminded of the barbaric overplus of jewelry which Clytemnestra had on her person in Strauss's *Elektra,* when she was cut to pieces by Orestes.

The point is that there were many artists who could transpose onto canvas the formal motifs of Art Nouveau jewelry, or who could raid the world of precious stones for new alliances of color, or who could go to turn-of-the-century architecture and interior design for new ideas about how to compose their pictures. The singularity of Klimt was that he could use these things as symbols, and in an emotional context of his own devising. It is worth remembering that Klimt's paintings were made at a time when pure Expressionism was the coming thing in Central Europe. Pure Expressionism is an art of immediate effect: all sense of distance is abolished, ideally, between the painter and his public. If people were shocked by Kirchner and his friends—or by Oskar Kokoschka, in Klimt's own city—it was precisely because of this abolition of all barriers. Klimt took down the bar-

riers, too, in one sense: no one was more direct than he about the nature of bodily attraction. But he multiplied the intensity of his insights by setting up, within the same image, a complex and luxurious flat patterning. That patterning had a life of its own; and it enabled Klimt to distance the human entanglements and to give them an air of redoubled fatality. Removed from the melodrama of everyday, they took on an emblematic quality: history as nightmare was taken out of the clinical report and given the antique resonance which it has in high art.

When it was clear that World War I would break out, it was natural that Expressionism should give nightmare literal form, as in the Apocalyptic Landscape series (fig. 44) of Ludwig Meidner. Meidner spoke of himself later as having been "driven to breaking-point by the approach of world catastrophe"; and his portraits of a great city in dissolution retain, even today, a certain descriptive force. But they have none of the mystery with which Caspar David Friedrich was able to invest a distant view of the town of Neubrandenburg going up in flames. Literalism does not last, in such a context; only the symbol survives. The apocalypse, when it came, was better interpreted by the ferocious and elliptic

46. (*above*) Pablo Picasso
The End of the Road, c. 1898
The Solomon R. Guggenheim Museum, New York

47. (*above right*) Arnold Böcklin
The Plague, 1898
Kunstmuseum, Basel

Symbols ideally should take us by surprise. Böcklin was a gifted painter and an exemplary craftsman, but in the last analysis his *The Plague* looks contrived and stagy: we do not forget that Böcklin was Swiss, and that Switzerland is the last country on earth where plague is likely to strike.

Picasso at age 16, though obviously gifted, had as yet nothing of his own to say in *The End of the Road,* and the image, though striking, might have been borrowed from one of the new magazines which came to Barcelona from all over Europe. It was left for the self-taught Henri Rousseau to give the 1890s a compelling and quite unpredictable symbol of the mindless and random afflictions which war brings everywhere with it.

48. (*left*) Henri Rousseau
War, c. 1895
The Museum of Modern Art, New York

49. Albert Pinkham Ryder
Death on a Pale Horse (or *The Race Track*)
The Cleveland Museum of Art

Ryder, a New Englander, was America's first truly visionary artist. In later years he became a shambling eccentric who lived in New York City, far from his beloved seacoast and yet serenely indifferent to the surrounding streets.

Death on a Pale Horse (or *The Race Track*) is said to have been prompted by the suicide of a friend who gambled his life savings on a horse race and lost.

methods of George Grosz, for one, in his *Metropolis,* 1917 (fig. 50). But it is with Max Beckmann that the concept of history as nightmare found a new fulfillment.

DISASTERS OUTWARD AND INWARD

Beckmann now looks to us like the predestined successor of the poets of disquiet with whom we have been dealing. In childhood and youth he was distinctly a member of the privileged classes. He was good-looking, self-confident and quite unusually precocious. His parents had a great deal of money and an assured position in society. In 1905, when he was 21, he became known throughout Germany for a large figure painting of *Young Men by the Sea.* He had the backing of two of the best judges of new painting in Europe, Count Harry Kessler and Henry van der Velde; he became a favorite with Paul Cassirer, then the most successful dealer in Berlin; and when Edvard Munch was in Berlin in 1906 it was only natural that Beckmann should be presented to him, as much for his sensational rise to fame as for the Munch-like overtones of *Young Men by the Sea.* (Beckmann, with his robust, outgoing nature, was none too pleased when Munch suggested to him that his real bent was for tragedy.) A self-portrait painted in Florence the following year shows a forthright, well-brushed young man in a high wing collar: a rising young lawyer or doctor, one might think, and in any case a man with nothing to hide and nothing to fear.

He was sensitive, even so, to the tormented inner life which is a part of the German heritage. He realized the full stature of Grünewald's Isenheim Altarpiece in Colmar at a time when that great painting found few to admire it, and in general he shared Kirchner's admiration for early German painting. It was from German Gothic, and not from his contemporaries, that he took the pure, thin, tart color, the confined shallow space, the needly, linear drawing and the overlapping zigzag of figures piled on top of one another that were to distinguish his paintings of 1917–20. German Gothic gave him the abrupt narrative style that enabled him to get through to the public of his day with a rare urgency; it also taught him to take the flesh off his paintings so that the map of feeling within them was exposed as if in a manual of anatomy.

Beckmann took some years to evolve this mature style; his subject matter, likewise, came along at its own pace and would not be hurried. He was concerned about what went on in the world—to the extent, in fact, of painting imaginary accounts of

50. George Grosz
Metropolis, 1917
The Museum of Modern Art, New York

George Grosz was 21 at the time of the outbreak of World War I. By the time he painted *Metropolis* he had been court-martialed for insubordination and narrowly escaped being shot. Best known for his wonderfully caustic and incisive drawings of a society in decay, he was also, as here, a gifted painter and a master analyst of big-city life.

events which he had not witnessed, like the earthquake in Messina (1908) and the loss of the *Titanic* (1912). But he treated these disasters very much from the outside, and as examples of broad, spectacular and manifestly "effective" subject matter. There is no reason to suppose that he saw them as symbols of anything in particular. But when World War I broke out, Beckmann had from the first a keen and sober understanding of what it meant. His *Declaration of War*, 1914 (fig. 52), is most revealing in this context. Beckmann set down in a spirit of complete objectivity the facts of what he had seen: that there were people in Germany who greeted the news of the outbreak of war in August, 1914, with bemusement, inertia and dread.

He himself went on to serve in the medical corps on the Russian front and in Flanders. It was at this point that history caught up with him, and the well-built, untroubled young man became a neurasthenic who had to be discharged from the army, after barely a year, as unfit for further service. When he began to paint again it was, as he said in 1917, "to reproach God for his errors." A great part of his new material came from the notes which he had taken during month after month of close contact with men who had been hideously wounded. This experience had given him a phantasmagorical insight into the casual indignities which come the way of the human body; and when the war came to an end in 1918, and it turned out that those indignities did not come to an end with it, Beckmann was able to sum up the situation in a big painting called *The Night* (fig. 51).

The Night is not an objective statement, like *Declaration of War*. It is a symbolic statement: "history as nightmare" is everywhere present in it. It has in it elements from the news of the day: the killing in furtive and underhand ways of people who should have played a lofty part in German life; the swinish conduct of the defeated military; the stealth with which evil deeds were done, and the readiness with which wicked men found accomplices, and the equanimity with which people would stand around and watch. All these things were a part of German life during the months—August, 1918, to March, 1919—that Beckmann toiled away at the picture; and it is, to that extent, a "document of the times." There is, in *The Night*, enough circumstantial detail to flesh out a novel; but the peculiar and lasting force of the picture is owed to its pre-echoes of an even more bestial era. This was how it would be when torture was taken for granted as the instrument of state policy, and when millions of people would live in dread of a knock on the door in the night. "You may live to see this" is the message of *The Night*. As in all Symbolist paintings of real quality, the artist spoke truer than he knew.

51. Max Beckmann
The Night, 1918–19
Kunstsammlung Nordrhein-Westfalen, Düsseldorf

52. Max Beckmann
Declaration of War, 1914
The Museum of Modern Art, New York

53. Max Beckmann
Operation, 1914
The Museum of Modern Art, New York

As a hospital orderly in an army that was sustaining heavy casualties, Beckmann spent much of every day in improvised operating rooms. Memorizing, as here, the look of bodies that have been torn apart, he brought himself in a very few months to the brink of nervous collapse.

It is not, however, a self-pitying picture. Beckmann's was not a negative nature. He believed that if the case was put in the right way, and with sufficient force, the course of history might just possibly be changed. But he did not underestimate the role of habit, and of ingrained obedience, in the German nature. In 1920, for instance, he painted his *Family Picture* (pl. XII): a portrait of an enclosed world, a shallow Gothic space updated to the 1920s and inhabited by six human beings, each one of them locked in his own concerns. These are the people who will have to choose, one way or the other; and as Beckmann himself lies brooding on the piano bench, the auguries do not look promising. His mother-in-law hides her face. His wife thinks only of the possible fading of her good looks. His sister-in-law has drifted into dreamland. The servant is content to sponge up the small print in the local newspaper. Beckmann's young son alone shows something of energy and resolution in the avidity with which he pores over his book. Elsewhere the concept of *Gemütlichkeit* has turned rancid.

Family Picture is not much fun to look at. As for *The Night*, it is one of the most disagreeable images which the art of our century has to show. Yet Beckmann nowhere exaggerates: he makes his

effects by enumeration, and by a certain steadiness of mind, and above all by the exact and unsparing draftsmanship which made him so fine a printmaker. One can admire these things and yet feel that these paintings bring bad news. What could be more rash, after all, than to assume that what happened in 1918–19, and what happened thereafter, will never happen again? If we have lived through even part of all that, we can be forgiven for not wanting to think about it. If we are young enough to know it only from hearsay, we are likely to have problems of our own time to preoccupy us. In either case, we may well be glad to let the ice reform over those particular seas. If all this were a matter of record—of keeping a particular body of knowledge in being— we could leave it to the libraries; art could find its material elsewhere. But what if the symbols which art has to offer are vital to our understanding of the world and cannot be found elsewhere? If that is so—and in the case of the works here discussed it is so, beyond a doubt—then what Kafka said about books is no less true about pictures. Here it is again: "What we need are books which come upon us like ill-fortune, and distress us deeply. . . . A book must be an ice axe, to break the sea frozen within us."

42

XII. Max Beckmann
Family Picture, 1920
The Museum of Modern Art, New York

SUGGESTED READINGS

Symbolism

Jung, Carl G. *Man and His Symbols.* Repr. 1964 ed.
    Garden City, N.Y., Doubleday, 1969.

Lövgren, Sven. *The Genesis of Modernism: Seurat, Gauguin, van Gogh and
    French Symbolism in the 1880s.* 2nd. rev. ed.
    Bloomington, Indiana, Indiana University Press, 1971.

Lucie-Smith, Edward. *Symbolist Art.*
    London, Thames and Hudson, 1972.

Milner, John. *Symbolists and Decadents.*
    London and New York, Studio Vista/Dutton Paperbacks, 1971.

Symons, Arthur. *The Symbolist Movement in Literature.*
    (First publ. 1899.) New York, Dutton, 1958.

Expressionism

Grohmann, Will. *Expressionists.*
    New York, Abrams, 1957.

Manvell, Roger, and Fraenkel, Heinrich. *The German Cinema.*
    New York, Praeger, 1971.

Miesel, Victor H., ed. *Voices of German Expressionism.*
    Englewood Cliffs, N.J., Prentice-Hall, 1970.

Myers, Bernard S. *The German Expressionists: A Generation in Revolt.*
    New York, McGraw-Hill, 1963.

Roethel, Hans K. *The Blue Rider.*
    New York, Praeger, 1972.

Roh, Franz. *German Art in the 20th Century.* Rev. ed.
    Greenwich, Conn., New York Graphic Society, 1968.

Selz, Peter. *German Expressionist Painting.*
    Berkeley and Los Angeles, University of California Press, 1957.

Max Beckmann

Kessler, Charles S. *Max Beckmann's Triptychs.*
    Cambridge, Mass., Belknap Press of Harvard University Press, 1970.

Selz, Peter. *Max Beckmann.*
    New York, The Museum of Modern Art, 1964.

Ernst Ludwig Kirchner

Gordon, Donald E. *Ernst Ludwig Kirchner.*
    Cambridge, Mass., Harvard University Press, 1968.

Grohmann, Will. *E. L. Kirchner.*
    New York, Arts Inc., 1961.

Gustav Klimt

Hofmann, Werner. *Gustav Klimt.*
    Greenwich, Conn., New York Graphic Society, 1972.

Gustave Moreau

Paladilhe, Jean, and Pierre, José. *Gustave Moreau.*
    New York, Praeger, 1972.

Edvard Munch

Benesch, Otto. *Edvard Munch.*
    London, Phaidon, 1960.

Heller, Reinhold. *Edvard Munch: The Scream.*
    New York, Viking, 1973.

Hodin, J. P. *Edvard Munch.*
    New York, Praeger, 1972.

Langaard, Johan H., and Revold, Reidar. *Edvard Munch: Masterpieces from
    the Artist's Collection in the Munch Museum in Oslo.*
    New York, Universe, 1972.

Messer, Thomas M. *Edvard Munch.*
    New York, Abrams, 1972.

Timm, Werner. *The Graphic Art of Edvard Munch.*
    Greenwich, Conn., New York Graphic Society, 1969.

Odilon Redon

Werner, Alfred. *The Graphic Works of Odilon Redon.*
    New York, Dover, 1969.

Auguste Rodin

Descharnes, Robert, and Chabrun, Jean-François. *Auguste Rodin.*
    New York, Viking, 1967.

Elsen, Albert Edward. *Rodin's Gates of Hell.*
    Minneapolis, University of Minnesota Press, 1960.

Elsen, Albert Edward. *Auguste Rodin: Readings on His Life and Work.*
    Englewood Cliffs, N.J., Prentice-Hall, 1965.

Sutton, Denys. *Triumphant Satyr: The World of Auguste Rodin.*
    New York, Hawthorne, 1966.

LIST OF ILLUSTRATIONS

Dimensions: height precedes width; a third dimension, depth, is given for sculptures and constructions where relevant. Foreign titles are in English, except in cases where the title does not translate or is better known in its original form. Asterisked titles indicate works reproduced in color.

Anonymous

Shawm Player, 1380 (fig. 30)
Bronze, 47 inches high
Germanisches Nationalmuseum, Nuremberg

Baldung, Hans (called Grien)
(1484/5–1545)

The Temptation of Eve (fig. 29)
Oil on panel, 25¼ x 13 inches
The National Gallery of Canada, Ottawa

Beckmann, Max
(1884–1950)

Declaration of War, 1914 (fig. 52)
Drypoint, 7¾ x 9¾ inches
The Museum of Modern Art, New York
Purchase

Operation, 1914 (fig. 53)
Drypoint, 11¾ x 17½ inches
The Museum of Modern Art, New York
Purchase

The Night, 1918–19 (fig. 51)
Oil on canvas, 53 x 61½ inches
Kunstsammlung Nordrhein-Westfalen, Düsseldorf

Family Picture, 1920 (pl. XII)
Oil on canvas, 25⅝ x 39¾ inches
The Museum of Modern Art, New York
Gift of Abby Aldrich Rockefeller

Böcklin, Arnold
(1827–1901)

The Plague, 1898 (fig. 47)
Tempera on wood, 59½ x 41½ inches
Kunstmuseum, Basel

Eickemeyer, Jr., Rudolf
(1862–1932)

"*In My Studio*" (Evelyn Nesbit on a bearskin rug), 1901 (fig. 40)
Photograph
Hudson River Museum, Yonkers, N.Y.

Friedrich, Caspar David
(1774–1840)

Self-Portrait, c. 1810 (fig. 2)
Drawing, 9 x 7 inches
Nationalgalerie, East Berlin

The Frozen Sea, 1822 (fig. 1)
Oil on canvas, 38½ x 46½ inches
Hamburger Kunsthalle, Hamburg

Gauguin, Paul
(1848–1903)

Portrait of Stéphane Mallarmé, 1891 (fig. 7)
Etching and drypoint, 7¼ x 5⅜ inches
The Museum of Modern Art, New York
Given anonymously

Goya, Francisco
(1746–1828)

The Colossus (or *Panic*), c. 1808 (fig. 3)
Oil on canvas, 45⅝ x 41⅜ inches
Museo del Prado, Madrid

Grosz, George
(1893–1959)

Metropolis, 1917 (fig. 50)
Oil on cardboard, 26¾ x 18¾ inches
The Museum of Modern Art, New York
Purchase (Stephen C. Clark Fund)

Heckel, Erich
(1883–1970)

The Village Dance, 1908 (fig. 24)
Oil on canvas, 26½ x 29½ inches
Nationalgalerie, Berlin

Walkers by the Grunewaldsee, 1911 (fig. 25)
Oil on canvas, 28¼ x 32¼ inches
Museum Folkwang, Essen

Two Men by a Table (scene from Dostoevsky's *The Idiot*), 1912 (fig. 26)
Oil on canvas, 38½ x 48 inches
Hamburger Kunsthalle, Hamburg

Herkomer, Hubert von
(1849–1914)

On Strike, 1891 (fig. 12)
Oil on canvas, 89¾ x 49¾ inches
Royal Academy of Arts, London

Kirchner, Ernst Ludwig
(1880–1938)

Wrestlers in a Circus, c. 1906–09 (fig. 33)
Oil on canvas, 31¾ x 37 inches
The Cleveland Museum of Art
Bequest of William R. Valentiner

Street, Dresden, 1907 (pl. VI)
Oil on canvas, 59¼ x 78⅞ inches
The Museum of Modern Art, New York
Purchase

Portrait of Erich Heckel, 1908 (fig. 23)
Oil on canvas, 48¾ x 26¾ inches
Städtisches Karl-Ernst-Osthaus-Museum, Hagen, Germany

Nude Dancers, 1909 (fig. 34)
Woodcut, 14⅜ x 20⅞ inches
The Museum of Modern Art, New York
Purchase

The Blue House in the Potholder District, 1909 (fig. 28)
Etching, 12 x 15⅝ inches
The Museum of Modern Art, New York
Larry Aldrich Fund

Panama Girls, 1910(?) (fig. 31)
Oil on canvas, 19¾ x 19¾ inches
North Carolina Museum of Art, Raleigh
Bequest of W. R. Valentiner

Standing Nude with Hat, 1910–20 (fig. 32)
Woodcut, 82 x 26 inches
Städtische Galerie, Frankfurt

Street, Berlin, 1913 (pl. VIII)
Oil on canvas, 47½ x 35⅞ inches
The Museum of Modern Art, New York
Purchase

Woman Buttoning Her Shoe, 1913(?) (fig. 27)
Woodcut, 12⅜ x 9⅞ inches
The Museum of Modern Art, New York
Larry Aldrich Fund (by exchange)

Klimt, Gustav
(1862–1918)

Study for "Philosophy," 1898–99 (fig. 36)
Drawing
Historisches Museum der Stadt, Vienna

Study for "Medicine," 1901 (fig. 37)
Drawing
Graphische Sammlung Albertina, Vienna

Judith I, 1901 (pl. IX)
Oil on canvas, 33½ x 16½ inches
Österreichische Galerie, Vienna

Portrait of Emilie Flöge, 1902 (pl. X)
Oil on canvas, 72¼ x 33½ inches
Historisches Museum der Stadt, Vienna

Water Serpents I, 1904–07 (pl. XI)
Mixed media on parchment, 20 x 8 inches
Österreichische Galerie, Vienna

Portrait of Margaret Stonborough-Wittgenstein,
1905 (fig. 42)
Oil on canvas, 72 x 36 inches
Neue Pinakothek, Munich

Danaë, 1907–08 (fig. 41)
Oil on canvas, 30½ x 33 inches
Private collection, Graz, Austria

Klinger, Max
(1857–1920)

The Glove, No. 9: "The Rape," 1878–80 (fig. 45)
from a series of 10 etchings, published by the
artist, Berlin, 1881 (Opus VI)
Etching, 4⅜ x 10¼ inches
The Museum of Modern Art, New York
Purchase

Kokoschka, Oskar
(b. 1886)

Cover design for *Der Sturm,* July 14, 1910 (fig. 43)
14¾ x 11⅜ inches
Private collection, London

Kollwitz, Käthe
(1867–1945)

Riot (Plate 5 from *The Weavers* cycle), 1897
(fig. 11)
Etching, 9 x 11½ inches
National Gallery of Art, Washington, D.C.

Mackintosh, Charles Rennie
(1868–1928)

The Scottish Musical Review, 1896 (fig. 38)
Lithograph, 97 x 39 inches
The Museum of Modern Art, New York
Acquired by exchange

Manet, Edouard
(1832–83)

Portrait of Stéphane Mallarmé, 1876 (fig. 5)
Oil on canvas, 10⅞ x 14¼ inches
Musée du Louvre, Paris

Meidner, Ludwig
(1884–1966)

Apocalyptic Mood, 1913 (fig. 44)
Pencil, 28⅛ x 18 inches
The St. Louis Art Museum
Gift of Morton D. May

Moreau, Gustave
(1826–98)

Oedipus and the Sphinx, 1864 (fig. 8)
Oil on canvas, 81¼ x 41¼ inches
The Metropolitan Museum of Art, New York
Bequest of William H. Herriman, 1921

Salome Dancing before Herod (detail), 1876
(pl. I)
Oil on canvas, 36½ x 24 inches
Musée Gustave Moreau, Paris

Munch, Edvard
(1863–1944)

Military Band on the Karl Johann Street, 1889
(fig. 20)
Oil on canvas, 56½ x 40 inches
Kunsthaus, Zürich

The Voice, 1893 (pl. III)
Oil on canvas, 34½ x 42½ inches
Museum of Fine Arts, Boston
Ernest Wadsworth Longfellow Fund

Ashes, 1894 (fig. 18)
Oil on canvas, 47½ x 55½ inches
Nasjonalgalleriet, Oslo

Woman, 1895 (fig. 17)
Drypoint and aquatint, 17¼ x 19½ inches
The Museum of Modern Art, New York
Acquired through the Lillie P. Bliss Bequest

Portrait of Stéphane Mallarmé, 1896 (fig. 6)
Etching, 22 x 28 inches
Museum of Fine Arts, Boston
Wm. Francis Warden Fund

Jealousy, 1896 (fig. 19)
Lithograph, 18¾ x 22⅝ inches
The Museum of Modern Art, New York
The William B. & Evelyn A. Jaffe Collection

Anxiety, 1896 (fig. 22)
Lithograph, 16⅜ x 15⅜ inches
The Museum of Modern Art, New York
Purchase

Program cover: *Solveig and Mother Aase,* 1896
(fig. 16)
Lithograph, 9½ x 11½ inches
The Brooklyn Museum, New York
Gift of Jean Goriany

Virginia Creeper, 1898 (pl. V)
Oil on cardboard, 47½ x 48¼ inches
Munch-museet, Oslo

The Dance of Life, 1899–1900 (pl. IV)
Oil on canvas, 50 x 76 inches
Nasjonalgalleriet, Oslo

Little Girls in Aasgaardstrand, 1904–05 (fig. 21)
Oil on cardboard, 34½ x 44¼ inches
Munch-museet, Oslo

Nolde, Emil
(1867–1956)

Solomon and His Wives, 1911 (fig. 35)
Etching and aquatint, 11⅞ x 9⅜ inches
The Museum of Modern Art, New York
Purchase

Picasso, Pablo
(1881–1973)

The End of the Road, c. 1898 (fig. 46)
Watercolor and conté crayon, 17⅞ x 11¾ inches
The Solomon R. Guggenheim Museum, New York
Courtesy of the Thannhauser Foundation

Redon, Odilon
(1840–1916)

Winged Head Flying over Sea, c. 1875 (fig. 10)
Charcoal on tan paper, 18¼ x 14⅝ inches
The Art Institute of Chicago
The David Adler Memorial Fund

The Masque of the Red Death, 1883 (fig. 9)
Charcoal on brown paper, 17¼ x 14⅛ inches
The Museum of Modern Art, New York
The John S. Newberry Collection

Roger and Angelica, c. 1910 (pl. II)
Pastel, 36½ x 28¾ inches
The Museum of Modern Art, New York
Lillie P. Bliss Collection

RKO Radio Pictures

King Kong, 1933 (fig. 4)
Film still
The Museum of Modern Art, New York
Film Stills Archive

Rodin, Auguste
(1840–1917)

The Earth, 1884 (fig. 15)
Bronze, 18⅛ x 41½ x 15 inches
B. G. Cantor Art Foundation, Beverly Hills,
    California

Gates of Hell, 1880–1917 (fig. 14)
Bronze, 20 feet 10¾ inches x 13 feet 2 inches x
    33⅜ inches
Philadelphia Museum of Art, Rodin Museum
Given by Jules E. Mastbaum

Detail, *Gates of Hell* (lower section of left door)
    (fig. 13)

Rousseau, Henri (called *le Douanier*)
(1844–1910)

War, c. 1895 (fig. 48)
Transfer lithograph, 8¾ x 13 inches
The Museum of Modern Art, New York
Given anonymously

Ryder, Albert Pinkham
(1847–1917)

Death on a Pale Horse (or The Race Track) (fig. 49)
Oil on canvas, 28¼ x 35¼ inches
The Cleveland Museum of Art
Purchase from the J. H. Wade Fund

Schmidt-Rottluff, Karl
(b. 1884)

Houses at Night, 1912 (pl. VII)
Oil on canvas, 37⅝ x 34½ inches
The Museum of Modern Art, New York
Gift of Mr. and Mrs. Walter Bareiss

Wright, Frank Lloyd
(1869–1959)

Windows (3), triptych: stained-glass leaded
    windows with wooden frame (fig. 39).
    Each 86¼ x 28 x 2 inches
The Metropolitan Museum of Art, New York
Purchase, 1967, Edward C. Moore, Jr., Gift
    and Edgar J. Kaufman Charitable Foundation
    Gift